Table of Contents

I0466843

The Author:

Hustle to the Top: A Modern Guide to Scaling Your Career Growth

Introduction:

Welcome to the hustle revolution, where ambition meets action, and dreams transform into reality! In today's fast-paced world, climbing the career ladder requires more than talent and luck—it demands hustle. But what exactly is hustle, you ask? It's the relentless drive to pursue your goals with passion, persistence, and a sprinkle of swagger. It's about seizing opportunities, embracing challenges, and refusing to settle for anything less than extraordinary.

There are no shortcuts or handouts in the hustle game—just hard work, determination, and a dash of hustle magic. It's about putting in the extra hours, making bold moves, and hustling smarter, not just harder. It's about stepping out of your comfort zone, taking risks, and defying the status quo. Let's face it: mediocrity is so last season, and average is not in our vocabulary.

But why is the career hustle so important? Well, picture this: you're at the starting line of your career journey, armed with ambition and a killer work ethic. You have big dreams and even bigger goals, but the road to success is paved with obstacles, naysayers, and countless detours. That's where hustle comes in—it's your secret weapon, your ace in the hole, your ticket to the top.

In today's hyper-competitive job market, standing out from the crowd is no easy feat. It takes more than just talent to get ahead—it takes hustle. Whether aiming for that coveted promotion, launching your startup, or chasing your wildest career dreams, hustle is the fuel that propels you forward. It's what sets the movers and shakers apart from the rest—it's the X factor that turns dreams into reality and ordinary into extraordinary.

So, if you're ready to level up your career game, it's time to unleash your inner hustler and show the world what you're made of. Get ready to hustle like never before because the only way to the top is through hard work, determination, and a whole lot of hustle. Strap in, buttercup, and let's hustle our way to the top!

Chapter 1: Hustle Mindset: Building Your Career Foundation

Embrace the Hustle Mentality

In a world where success stories often seem like overnight sensations, it's easy to overlook the gritty, behind-the-scenes hustle that propels individuals to greatness. But make no mistake—the hustle mentality is the secret sauce that separates the dreamers from the doers, the spectators from the game-changers. So what exactly does it mean to hustle, and why is it essential for achieving career success?

To hustle is to embody a mindset of relentless determination, unwavering perseverance, and boundless ambition. It's about rolling up your sleeves, diving headfirst into challenges, and refusing to take no for an answer. It's the burning desire to push past obstacles, exceed expectations, and shatter limitations. It's the refusal to settle for mediocrity and the unwavering belief that greatness is within reach—if only you're willing to hustle for it.

But hustle is more than just a buzzword or a trendy catchphrase—it's a way of life, a philosophy that permeates every aspect of your career journey. It's about embracing the grind, embracing the hustle, and embracing the journey, no matter how long or winding the road may be. Let's face it—success rarely happens overnight, and overnight sensations are often years in the making. It's the daily hustle—the small victories, the setbacks, the breakthroughs—that ultimately pave the way to greatness.

So why is embracing the hustle mentality essential for achieving career success? For starters, it's the ultimate equalizer—the one thing anyone can control regardless of background or circumstance. In a world where talent and opportunities are plentiful, hustle sets you apart. The X factor turns potential into performance and ambition into achievement.

Perhaps more importantly, embracing the hustle mentality is essential for cultivating resilience, grit, and self-reliance—the qualities indispensable for navigating the inevitable ups and downs of the career journey. In a world where success is never guaranteed and failure is always possible, hustlers refuse to give up and are deterred by setbacks, ultimately coming out on top.

You can take your career to the next level, but it's time to embrace the hustle mentality with open arms. Roll up your sleeves, dig deep, and get ready to hustle like never before—because the road to success is paved with hustle, and the journey is just beginning. Go ahead—embrace the hustle, embrace the grind, and embrace the journey. Your future self will thank you for it.

Tips for Setting Ambitious Yet Achievable Career Goals & Staying Motivated On Your Journey
Setting ambitious yet achievable career goals is the cornerstone of success in today's competitive landscape. But with so many possibilities and potential paths to pursue, it can be overwhelming to know where to begin. That's why it's essential to approach goal-setting with clarity, intentionality, and a healthy dose of realism. Here are some tips to help you set ambitious yet achievable career goals and stay motivated on your journey:

Start with the end in mind: Before you can set meaningful career goals, it's essential to have a clear vision of where you want to end up. Take some time to reflect on your long-term personal and professional aspirations. What does success look like to you? What are your ultimate career objectives? By starting with the end in mind, you can work backward to identify the steps needed to get there.

Make them SMART: When setting career goals, it's crucial to make them SMART—specific, measurable, achievable, relevant, and time-bound. Instead of vague aspirations like "get promoted" or "earn more money," aim for concrete objectives such as "earn a promotion to [specific position] within the next two years" or "increase my annual income by 20% within the next five years." This will give you a clear roadmap and tangible metrics to track your progress.

Break them into smaller milestones: Big goals can feel daunting, so it's essential to break them down into smaller, more manageable milestones. Divide your long-term objectives into bite-sized tasks or milestones that you can tackle individually. Celebrate each small victory along the way, and use them as motivation to keep pushing forward.

Stay flexible and adaptable: While setting ambitious goals is essential, remaining flexible and versatile in unexpected challenges or opportunities is crucial. Your career journey may only sometimes follow a straight line, and that's okay. Be willing to adjust your goals as needed, pivot when necessary, and embrace unexpected twists and turns.

Find your why: Motivation is the fuel that drives you toward your goals, so it's essential to understand your "why" behind each objective. What motivates you to pursue these goals? How will achieving them impact your life and career? Whether it's a desire for personal growth, financial security, or a sense of purpose, knowing your why will help keep you focused and driven, even when the going gets tough.

Surround yourself with support: Building a solid support network of mentors, peers, and cheerleaders can make all the difference in staying motivated on your career journey. Surround yourself with people who believe in you, challenge you, and inspire you to be your best self. Lean on them for advice, encouragement, and accountability when needed.

Practice self-care: Finally, remember to prioritize self-care along the way. Balancing ambition with self-care is essential for maintaining your physical, mental, and emotional well-being, which are critical to long-term success. Take breaks when needed, prioritize activities that bring you joy and fulfillment, and don't be afraid to ask for help when needed.

By following these tips for setting ambitious yet achievable career goals and staying motivated, you'll be well-equipped to turn your aspirations into reality and achieve your desired success. Dream big, work hard, and never lose sight of the incredible potential that lies within you. Let me repeat this. Your future self will thank you for it.

Strategies for Developing A Growth Mindset and Overcoming Obstacles With Resilience and Determination
In the ever-evolving landscape of the modern workforce, possessing a growth mindset is not just advantageous—it's essential for thriving amidst constant change and challenges. A growth mindset believes in one's ability to learn, grow, and improve, regardless of setbacks or obstacles. It's about embracing challenges as opportunities for growth, viewing failure as a stepping stone to success, and approaching life with curiosity, resilience, and determination. Here are some strategies for developing a growth mindset and overcoming obstacles with resilience and determination:

Embrace challenges as opportunities: Instead of shying away from challenges or viewing them as insurmountable obstacles, embrace them as opportunities for growth and learning. Adopting a mindset of "I can't do it yet, but I will figure it out" can help shift your perspective and empower you to tackle even the most daunting tasks with confidence and determination.

Cultivate a love for learning: A growth mindset is all about continuous improvement and lifelong learning. Make a habit of seeking new experiences, acquiring new skills, and expanding your knowledge base. Whether through formal education, online courses, or self-directed study, prioritize learning as a central part of your personal and professional development journey.

Reframe failure as feedback: Instead of viewing failure as a final verdict on your abilities, see it as valuable feedback that can inform future success. Every setback presents an opportunity to learn, grow, and refine your approach. Ask yourself: What can I learn from this experience? How can I use this feedback to improve in the future? Reframing failure as a natural part of the learning process, you can develop resilience and bounce back more vital than ever.

Practice self-compassion: Developing a growth mindset requires a healthy dose of self-compassion and self-acceptance. Be kind to yourself, especially in the face of setbacks or failures. Treat yourself with the same kindness and understanding you would offer to a friend facing similar challenges. Remember that nobody is perfect, and mistakes are inevitable in the journey toward growth and success.

Cultivate a support network: Surround yourself with people who believe in you, support your goals, and encourage your growth. Seek mentors, coaches, and peers who can offer guidance, feedback, and perspective. Lean on your support network for encouragement and motivation when faced with obstacles or setbacks, and be willing to provide support in return.

Set realistic goals and celebrate progress: Break your long-term goals into smaller, more manageable milestones, and celebrate each step of the journey. By setting realistic goals and acknowledging your progress, you can stay motivated and focused on your ultimate objectives. Remember that growth takes time, and every small victory brings you one step closer to your goals.

Cultivate resilience: Finally, cultivate resilience—the ability to bounce back from setbacks, adapt to change, and persevere in adversity. Resilience is a critical component of a growth mindset, enabling you to weather the inevitable storms of life and emerge stronger on the other side. Practice mindfulness, cultivate gratitude, and develop coping strategies that help you navigate challenges gracefully and resiliently.

By implementing these strategies for developing a growth mindset and overcoming obstacles with resilience and determination, you can unlock your full potential and achieve success in both your personal and professional life. Remember that growth is a journey, not a destination, and overcoming each obstacle brings you one step closer to realizing your dreams. Embrace the challenges, cultivate resilience, and keep striving for greatness. The sky's the limit!

Chapter 2: Personal Branding 101: Make Yourself Stand Out

Define Personal Branding and Its Role in Career Advancement
In today's interconnected world, personal branding has emerged as a powerful tool for professionals looking to stand out in a crowded marketplace and advance their careers. But what exactly is personal branding, and why is it crucial for career advancement?

At its core, personal branding is the art of shaping and managing how others perceive you. It encompasses everything from your professional reputation and online presence to your unique skills, values, and personality traits. In essence, your brand sets you apart from your peers—it makes you memorable, distinctive, and indispensable in the eyes of employers, clients, and colleagues.

But personal branding is more than just crafting a catchy tagline or designing a sleek logo—it's about authentically showcasing who you are and what you bring to the table. It's about identifying your strengths, passions, and areas of expertise and leveraging them to create a compelling narrative that resonates with your target audience. Whether you're a seasoned executive, a budding entrepreneur, or a recent graduate just starting your career, your brand is your most valuable asset—it's what opens doors, creates opportunities, and propels you toward success.

So why is personal branding so crucial for career advancement? In today's hyper-competitive job market, having a solid personal brand can be the difference between landing your dream job and getting lost in the shuffle. Employers are inundated with resumes and LinkedIn profiles, and standing out from the crowd requires more than just a stellar CV or impressive credentials—it requires a compelling personal brand that sets you apart from the competition.

But personal branding isn't just about getting noticed—it's also about building trust, credibility, and authority in your chosen field. You establish yourself as a thought leader and go-to expert in your niche when you consistently deliver value, showcase your expertise, and engage with your audience meaningfully. This attracts new opportunities and clients and positions you as a valuable asset within your organization, paving the way for career advancement and growth.

Furthermore, personal branding empowers you to take control of your professional destiny and shape your career on your terms. Instead of waiting for opportunities to come to you, you can proactively create them by strategically positioning yourself in the marketplace, nurturing relationships with key influencers, and actively promoting your brand across various channels. Whether you're aiming for a promotion, exploring new career opportunities, or launching your own business, your brand serves as your compass, guiding you toward your goals and helping you navigate the ever-changing landscape of the modern workforce.

Ultimately, personal branding is not just a buzzword or a passing trend—it's a strategic imperative for professionals looking to thrive in today's competitive job market. By defining and cultivating your brand, you can differentiate yourself from the competition, build credibility and authority in your field, and create new career and growth opportunities. Invest in your brand, nurture it like its valuable asset, and watch as doors open, opportunities abound, and your career takes flight.

Tips for Crafting A Unique Personal Brand That Reflects Your Skills, Values, and Aspirations
Crafting a unique personal brand is more than just slapping a logo on your LinkedIn profile or coming up with a catchy tagline—it's about authentically showcasing who you are, what you stand for, and what you bring to the table. Your brand is your digital calling card, professional reputation, and a ticket to standing out in a crowded marketplace. Here are some tips for crafting a personal brand that reflects your skills, values, and aspirations:

Start with self-reflection: Before effectively crafting your brand, you need to understand who you are and what you stand for clearly. Take some time for self-reflection to identify your strengths, passions, values, and long-term goals. What are you passionate about? What unique skills or experiences do you bring to the table? What impact do you want to make in your industry or community? You can begin defining your personal brand's essence by answering these questions.

Pause, let that sink in...

Define your target audience: Like any brand, you should tailor your brand to resonate with a specific audience. Consider who you are trying to reach—potential employers, clients, colleagues, or industry peers—and what they value most. What challenges are they facing? What are their pain points? How can you position yourself as the solution to their needs? Understanding your target audience can tailor your messaging and positioning to speak directly to their interests and aspirations.

You already know to Pause here...

Showcase your unique value proposition: What sets you apart from the competition? What makes you uniquely qualified to solve your target audience's problems? Your unique value proposition (UVP) is the foundation of your brand—it's what makes you stand out in a sea of sameness. Identify your key strengths, skills, and experiences, and highlight them prominently in your branding materials. Whether it's your industry expertise, innovative approach to problem-solving, or passion for making a difference, make sure your UVP shines through in everything you do.

Perhaps a little thought?

Be authentic and consistent: Authenticity is the cornerstone of a solid personal brand. Your brand should genuinely reflect who you are—not who you think you should be. Be genuine, transparent, and authentic to yourself in all of your interactions and communications. Don't try to be someone you're not, or you'll risk being inauthentic and insincere. Additionally, consistency is critical to building brand recognition and trust. Ensure that your brand is consistent across all your online and offline channels, from your social media profiles to your resume to your networking interactions.

Tell your story: Storytelling is a powerful tool for building connections and engaging your audience emotionally. Use your brand to tell your story compellingly and authentically. Share your journey, successes, failures, and lessons learned. Be vulnerable, relatable, and human. By sharing your authentic story, you can create a deeper connection with your audience and establish yourself as a trusted authority in your field.

Invest in your online presence: In today's digital age, your online presence plays a crucial role in shaping your brand. Take the time to optimize your LinkedIn profile, create a professional website or blog, and actively engage with your audience on social media. Share valuable content, participate in industry discussions, and showcase your expertise through articles, videos, or podcasts.

Additionally, be mindful of your online reputation and how you present yourself online. Google yourself regularly to see what publicly available information about you is available, and take steps to manage your online presence accordingly.

Seek feedback and iterate: Building a personal brand is an ongoing process that requires continuous refinement and iteration. Seek feedback from trusted mentors, peers, and colleagues, and be open to constructive criticism. Use this feedback to identify areas for improvement and refine your brand accordingly. Additionally, regularly evaluate the effectiveness of your personal branding efforts and make adjustments as needed to ensure that your brand remains relevant and resonant with your target audience.

Crafting a unique personal brand that reflects your skills, values, and aspirations is a powerful way to differentiate yourself in today's competitive marketplace. By following these tips and investing the time and effort to build and maintain your brand, you can position yourself for success and unlock new career and growth opportunities. Embrace your uniqueness, tell your story, and let your brand shine bright!

Leveraging Social Media and Online Platforms to Showcase Your Expertise and Expand Your Professional Network
In today's digital age, social media and online platforms have become powerful tools for professionals looking to showcase their expertise, expand their professional network, and advance their careers. Whether you're a seasoned executive, a budding entrepreneur, or a recent graduate just starting your career, leveraging social media and online platforms can help you build your brand, establish thought leadership, and create new growth opportunities. Here are some strategies for leveraging social media and online platforms to showcase your expertise and expand your professional network:

Choose the right platforms: With so many social media platforms and online channels, focusing your efforts on the most relevant to your industry and target audience is essential. Whether LinkedIn for professional networking, Twitter for industry news and insights, or Instagram for visual storytelling, choose platforms that align with your goals and where your target audience is most active.

Optimize your profiles: Your social media profiles are often the first impression people will have of you online, so making them count is crucial. Ensure your profiles are complete, professional, and up-to-date, with a clear and compelling bio highlighting your expertise, skills, and accomplishments. Use high-quality, professional photos, and customize your profile settings to maximize visibility and engagement.

Share valuable content: Content is king on social media, so share helpful, relevant content that showcases your expertise and provides value to your audience. Whether it's industry insights, thought leadership articles, case studies, or tips and advice, share content that positions you as a knowledgeable authority in your field and sparks conversation and engagement with your audience.

Engage with your audience: Social media is about building relationships and fostering engagement, so be proactive about engaging with your audience. Respond to comments and messages promptly, participate in industry discussions and forums, and share and comment on content from others in your network. By actively engaging with your audience, you can build trust, credibility, and rapport and expand your professional network organically.

Showcase your work: Social media and online platforms provide an excellent opportunity to showcase your work and accomplishments to a broad audience. Whether it's sharing project updates, client testimonials, or portfolio pieces, use these platforms to highlight your skills and expertise and demonstrate the value you bring to the table. Visual content such as videos, infographics, and presentations can effectively showcase your work compellingly and engagingly.

Network strategically: Social media and online platforms offer endless networking opportunities, but it's essential to approach networking strategically. Be intentional about connecting with professionals in your industry, including colleagues, mentors, influencers, and potential collaborators. Personalize your connection requests and engage in meaningful conversations to build genuine relationships and foster mutual support and collaboration.

Stay active and consistent: Building a solid presence on social media and online platforms requires consistency and dedication. Make it a habit to post regularly, engage with your audience consistently, and stay active in industry conversations and communities. Set aside dedicated time each day or week to manage your social media presence, curate content, and engage with your network. You can maintain momentum and grow your presence and influence online by staying active and consistent.

In general, leveraging social media and online platforms can be a game-changer for professionals looking to showcase their expertise, expand their professional network, and advance their careers. By following these strategies and investing the time and effort to build and maintain your online presence, you can position yourself as a trusted authority in your field, connect with like-minded professionals, and unlock new opportunities for growth and success. Don't wait—get out there, start sharing, and let your expertise shine online!

Chapter 3: Networking Like a Boss: Building Meaningful Connections

The art of networking in today's digital age: from LinkedIn to networking events and beyond

In today's interconnected world, networking has evolved from traditional face-to-face interactions to include a diverse array of digital platforms and online communities. Whether you're a seasoned professional, a recent graduate, or an aspiring entrepreneur, mastering the art of networking in today's digital age is essential for building relationships, expanding your professional network, and advancing your career. From LinkedIn to networking events and beyond, here's how to navigate the digital networking landscape with finesse and effectiveness:

LinkedIn: Your Digital Rolodex: LinkedIn has emerged as the go-to platform for professional networking in the digital age. With over 700 million users worldwide, it offers many opportunities to connect with colleagues, industry peers, potential employers, and clients. Ensure your LinkedIn profile is complete, professional, and optimized with relevant keywords and skills. Join industry groups and participate in discussions to expand your network and demonstrate your expertise. Don't hesitate to contact professionals you admire for informational interviews or mentorship opportunities.

Networking Events: Virtually and In-Person: While in-person networking events may have taken a backseat recently, virtual networking events have surged in popularity. Whether it's industry conferences, webinars, or virtual meetups, these events offer valuable opportunities to connect with like-minded professionals worldwide. Prepare by researching the event agenda, speakers, and attendees, and set specific networking goals for yourself. Be proactive about introducing yourself, engaging in conversations, and following up with new contacts afterward to maintain the connection.

Social Media Platforms: Beyond LinkedIn: While LinkedIn is a powerful platform for professional networking, pay attention to the networking potential of other social media platforms such as Twitter, Facebook, and Instagram. Follow industry influencers, participate in Twitter chats, and join Facebook groups related to your field to expand your network and stay informed about industry trends and opportunities. Share valuable content, engage with your audience, and showcase your expertise to attract like-minded professionals and foster meaningful connections.

Online Communities and Forums: Niche Networking: From industry-specific forums to niche online communities, there are countless digital spaces where professionals gather to exchange ideas, share resources, and connect with others in their field. Whether it's Reddit communities, Slack channels, or specialized forums, seek out online communities relevant to your interests and expertise. Participate in discussions, offer insights and advice, and build relationships with fellow members to expand your network and stay connected to the pulse of your industry.

Informational Interviews: Building Relationships: Informational interviews are a valuable networking tool for gaining insights into different industries, roles, and career paths while building meaningful relationships with professionals in your field. Reach out to professionals you admire and request a brief informational interview to learn more about their career journey, industry insights, and advice for aspiring professionals. Respect their time, come prepared with thoughtful questions, and express gratitude for their insights afterward.

Follow-Up and Nurture Relationships: Building a solid professional network isn't just about making connections—it's about nurturing and maintaining those relationships over time. Follow up with new contacts promptly after networking events or digital interactions to express gratitude, reinforce the connection, and continue the conversation. Stay in touch with your network regularly through personalized messages, updates, and occasional check-ins to keep the relationship alive and demonstrate your genuine interest and appreciation.

Mastering the art of networking in today's digital age requires a blend of online savvy, proactive engagement, and genuine relationship-building skills. Whether you're leveraging LinkedIn, attending virtual networking events, or engaging with online communities, approach networking with authenticity, curiosity, and a willingness to add value to others. By cultivating meaningful connections, expanding your professional network, and staying engaged in your industry, you can unlock new opportunities, advance your career, and thrive in the digital networking landscape. Get out there, make connections, and let your network be your greatest asset in achieving your professional goals.

Strategies for Building and Nurturing Genuine Relationships with Industry Peers, Mentors, and Potential Collaborators

Building and nurturing genuine relationships with industry peers, mentors, and potential collaborators is essential for professional growth, learning, and advancement. In today's interconnected world, success often depends as much on the strength of your network as it does on your skills and expertise. Here are some strategies for building and nurturing genuine relationships with industry peers, mentors, and potential collaborators:

Be Authentic and Genuine: Authenticity is the foundation of any meaningful relationship. Be yourself, be genuine, and show sincere interest in getting to know others. People can sense when you're authentic and are more likely to trust and connect with you when you're genuine. Don't be afraid to share your successes, challenges, and vulnerabilities—often, these shared experiences form the basis of solid connections.

Listen and Show Empathy: Effective communication is a two-way street; listening is as critical as speaking. Practice active listening by giving others your full attention, asking thoughtful questions, and showing genuine interest in their experiences and perspectives. Empathize with their challenges, celebrate their successes, and offer support and encouragement whenever possible. Being a good listener and showing empathy can deepen your connections and build trust with others.

Offer Value and Support: Building relationships is not just about what you can get—it's also about what you can give. Look for opportunities to offer value and support to your industry peers, mentors, and potential collaborators. Share your knowledge, expertise, and resources generously, offer help and assistance whenever needed, and be proactive about contributing to the success of others. Adding value to other's lives and careers will naturally attract like-minded individuals who appreciate your contributions and are eager to reciprocate.

Be Consistent and Reliable: Consistency and reliability are vital in building trust and credibility in your relationships. Follow your commitments, deliver on your promises, and be there for others when they need you. Stay in touch with your industry peers, mentors, and potential collaborators through personalized messages, updates, and occasional check-ins. By being consistent and reliable, you'll demonstrate your integrity and dedication, essential qualities for fostering solid and lasting relationships.

Seek Out Common Ground: Look for common interests, goals, and values you share with your industry peers, mentors, and potential collaborators. Whether it's a shared passion for a particular industry trend, a typical career aspiration, or a mutual desire to make a positive impact, finding common ground can help strengthen your connection and provide a solid foundation for collaboration and partnership. Be proactive about finding opportunities to connect personally and cultivate shared experiences that deepen your bond.

Be Open to Feedback and Growth: Building genuine relationships requires a willingness to learn, grow, and adapt. Be open to feedback from your industry peers, mentors, and potential collaborators, and use it as an opportunity for self-reflection and improvement. Be humble enough to admit you're wrong, take constructive criticism in stride, and use it for personal and professional growth. Demonstrating a growth mindset and a willingness to learn from others will build trust and respect in your relationships and create a supportive environment for mutual growth and development.

Building and nurturing genuine relationships with industry peers, mentors, and potential collaborators is essential for professional success and fulfillment. By being authentic, listening empathetically, offering value and support, being consistent and reliable, seeking common ground, and being open to feedback and growth, you can cultivate meaningful connections that enrich your career journey and open doors to new opportunities. Invest in your relationships, nurture them with care and intentionality, and watch as they become a source of inspiration, support, and growth throughout your career.

Tips for Effective Follow-Up and Maintaining Connections for Long-Term Career Growth
Effective follow-up and maintaining connections are crucial to nurturing relationships for long-term career growth. In today's fast-paced world, where attention spans are short, and competition is fierce, staying top-of-mind with your network can make all the difference in advancing your career and seizing new opportunities. Here are some tips for effective follow-up and maintaining connections for long-term career growth:

Be Prompt and Timely: Timing is everything when it comes to follow-up. Respond promptly to emails, messages, and requests from your network. Whether it's a follow-up after a networking event, a response to an email inquiry, or a thank-you note after a meeting, aim to reply within 24-48 hours to demonstrate your professionalism and responsiveness. By being timely in your follow-up, you show respect for others' time and reinforce your commitment to building and maintaining relationships.

Personalize Your Communication: Generic, one-size-fits-all follow-up messages are unlikely to make a lasting impression. Instead, personalize your communication with each individual in your network. Reference specific conversations, shared experiences, or mutual interests to show that you value the relationship and remember the details. Whether it's a personalized email, a handwritten note, or a thoughtful comment on social media, make your communication stand out by tailoring it to the recipient.

Provide Value and Support: Effective follow-up is not just about checking in—it's also about providing value and support to your network. Look for opportunities to offer assistance, share resources, or provide insights relevant to your contacts' interests and goals. Whether making an introduction, sharing a relevant article, or offering advice based on your expertise, be proactive about adding value to your network's lives and careers. By being a valuable resource, you'll deepen your connections and strengthen your relationships over time.

Stay Engaged and Consistent: Maintaining connections for long-term career growth requires ongoing effort and engagement. Stay active and consistent in communicating with your network, whether through regular emails, social media interactions, or occasional check-ins. Set aside dedicated time each week to nurture your relationships, reach out to contacts you last spoke to a while ago, and stay informed about their activities and achievements. You'll demonstrate your commitment to building meaningful connections by staying engaged and consistent.

Follow-Up with a Purpose: Effective follow-up is not just about staying in touch for the sake of it—it's about following up with a purpose. Before contacting a contact, consider what you hope to achieve from the interaction. Whether seeking advice, exploring potential collaboration opportunities, or simply catching up, have a clear objective in mind and tailor your follow-up accordingly. By being intentional about your follow-up, you'll make the most of your interactions and ensure they mutually benefit both parties.

Keep Track of Your Network: With a growing network, losing track of who and when you last connected is easy. Keep a record of your contacts, including their names, contact information, and critical details about your interactions. Use a CRM system, a spreadsheet, or a notebook to organize your network and track your follow-up efforts. Set reminders to contact contacts periodically to stay top-of-mind and maintain the connection over time.

Be Genuine and Authentic: Be genuine and authentic in your interactions with your network. Building and maintaining relationships is about building trust, and authenticity is the foundation of faith. Be sincere in your communication, show genuine interest in others, and be transparent about your intentions. People can sense when you're insincere or opportunistic, so always prioritize building genuine connections based on mutual respect and trust.

Considering everything, effective follow-up and maintaining connections are essential for long-term career growth and success. By being prompt and timely, personalizing your communication, providing value and support, staying engaged and consistent, following up with a purpose, keeping track of your network, and being genuine and authentic, you can cultivate meaningful relationships that will support you throughout your career journey. Invest in your network, nurture your connections with care and intentionality, and watch as they become a source of inspiration, support, and opportunity for years.

Chapter 4: Self-Promotion Strategies: Shine Bright Like a Diamond

Overcoming Imposter Syndrome and Confidently Promoting Your Achievements and Expertise

Hey there, superstar! Let's talk about something we all deal with but might not always want to admit: imposter syndrome. That sneaky voice in your head that whispers, "You're not good enough," or "You don't belong here." Well, guess what? It's time to kick imposter syndrome to the curb and start owning your greatness like the boss you are!

First, recognize that imposter syndrome is typical. Some of the most successful people have dealt with it at some point in their careers. Cut yourself some slack and know you're not alone in feeling this way.

Now, let's talk about how to overcome imposter syndrome and confidently promote your achievements and expertise:

Own Your Successes: You've worked hard to get where you are, so own it! Celebrate your wins, big and small, and give yourself credit where credit is due. Remember, you didn't get to where you are by luck—through hard work, determination, and much hustle.

Change Your Inner Dialogue: Instead of listening to that negative voice telling you you're not good enough, replace it with positive affirmations. Remember your accomplishments and skills and why you deserve to be where you are. You've got this!

Surround Yourself with Support: Don't be afraid to lean on your tribe when imposter syndrome starts rearing its ugly head. Surround yourself with people who believe in you, support you, and lift you when you are feeling down—solid support, whether friends, family, mentors, or colleagues, can make all the difference.

Embrace Your Uniqueness: Instead of trying to fit into someone else's mold of success, embrace what makes you unique. Own your quirks, passions, and individuality, and let them shine through in everything you do. Remember, your differences make you stand out and bring value.

Practice Self-Compassion: When imposter syndrome starts creeping in, cut yourself slack and practice self-compassion. Treat yourself with the same kindness and understanding you would offer a friend facing similar doubts. Remember, nobody's perfect, and cutting yourself some slack occasionally is okay.

Keep Pushing Yourself: Don't let imposter syndrome prevent you from reaching your full potential. Keep pushing yourself out of your comfort zone, taking on new challenges, and pushing the boundaries of what you think you're capable of. The more you challenge yourself, the more you realize how capable and deserving you are.

So, there you have some tips for overcoming imposter syndrome and confidently promoting your achievements and expertise. Remember, you're a total rockstar; the world deserves to see it! Go out there, own your greatness, and show the world what you're made of. You've got this!

Crafting a Compelling Elevator Pitch and Mastering the Art of Self-Promotion in Various Professional Settings
Alright, picture this: you step into an elevator, and just as the doors are about to close, in walks your dream client, investor, or future employer. You have about 30 seconds to make a killer first impression and sell yourself like your boss. That's where your elevator pitch comes in—a short, sweet, and oh-so-compelling introduction that leaves them wanting more.

Crafting a killer elevator pitch is about distilling your story, value proposition, and unique selling points into a bite-sized package that grabs attention and leaves a lasting impression. Let's break it down and master the art of self-promotion in various professional settings:

Keep It Short and Sweet: Your elevator pitch should be no more than 30-60 seconds long—just long enough to make your point without losing their interest. Start with a hook to grab their attention, then quickly introduce yourself and your expertise, and wrap it up with a call to action or a question to keep the conversation flowing.

Know Your Audience: Tailor your elevator pitch to your audience and the specific context you're in. Whether you're pitching to a potential client, investor, employer, or networking contact, speak their language and highlight the aspects of your background and experience most relevant to them. Show them how you can solve their problems or help them achieve their goals, and watch their eyes light up with interest.

Highlight Your Unique Selling Points: What sets you apart from the crowd? Whether it's your unique skills, experiences, or achievements, highlight your USPs in your elevator pitch. What makes you the best person for the job or the perfect fit for their needs? Don't be shy about singing your praises—you've worked hard to get where you are, so own it!

Practice, Practice, Practice: Like any good pitch, practice makes perfect. Take the time to rehearse your elevator pitch until it rolls off your tongue effortlessly. Practice in front of the mirror, with friends or family, or even record yourself and listen back to fine-tune your delivery. The more you practice, the more confident and polished you'll be when the moment of truth arrives.

Be Authentic and Passionate. Your elevator pitch should reflect who you are and your passion. Let your personality shine, and don't be afraid to inject enthusiasm and energy into your delivery. After all, love is contagious, and people are drawn to those genuinely excited about what they do.

Follow Up and Keep the Conversation Going: Once you've delivered your killer elevator pitch, don't let the conversation end there. Follow up with a friendly email or LinkedIn message to thank them for their time and express your interest in continuing the conversation. Whether it leads to a meeting, a coffee chat, or a new opportunity, keeping the conversation going is vital to building lasting connections and advancing your career.

With a killer elevator pitch in your back pocket, you'll be ready to seize any opportunity that comes your way and take your career to new heights. Go ahead, rock that elevator pitch like the boss you are, and watch as doors start opening left and right. You've got this!

Using storytelling Techniques to Captivate Your Audience and Leave a Lasting Impression

Alright, buckle up because we're about to dive into the world of storytelling—a powerful tool for captivating your audience, making a lasting impression, and bringing your message to life like never before. Whether you're pitching a new idea, presenting, or networking at an event, storytelling can take your communication skills to the next level and leave your audience hanging on your every word.

So, what's the secret sauce behind a compelling story? It's all about tapping into your audience's emotions, experiences, and aspirations and taking them on a journey they'll never forget. But don't just take my word for it—let me show you a couple of stories to drive home the point:

Story #1: The Underdog Triumphs

Once upon a time, there was a young entrepreneur named Maya in a bustling city full of hustle and bustle. Maya had a big dream—to launch her sustainable fashion brand—but faced countless obstacles. From securing funding to finding suppliers to building a customer base, the road to success was anything but smooth.

But Maya was determined to make her dream a reality, and she refused to give up, no matter how many times she stumbled and fell. She poured her heart and soul into her business, working late into the night and sacrificing weekends and holidays to make it happen.

And you know what? All that hard work paid off. Despite the odds stacked against her, Maya's sustainable fashion brand took off like wildfire, capturing the hearts and minds of consumers around the world. Today, Maya is living her dream, positively impacting the planet, and inspiring others to follow their passions no matter what.

Story #2: The Power of Collaboration

Picture this: a group of strangers brought together by chance at a networking event in the city's heart. Among them is Alex, a freelance graphic designer with big dreams and ambitions. As Alex mingles with the crowd, exchanging business cards and small talk, he can't help but feel a sense of excitement and possibility in the air.

Suddenly, Alex starts a conversation with Sarah, a fellow creative with a knack for storytelling. As they chat, they realize they share a common goal—to launch a collaborative project that combines their talents and passions uniquely and positively.

Before they know it, Alex and Sarah brainstorm ideas, bounce concepts off each other, and ignite creative sparks illuminating the room. Together, they hatch a plan to create a multimedia campaign that raises awareness about mental health issues and promotes self-care and self-expression through art and storytelling.

And you know what? With their combined powers, Alex and Sarah's project became a smashing success, touching hearts, sparking conversations, and making a real difference in those struggling with mental health challenges. And it all started with a chance encounter and a shared vision for a brighter, more compassionate world.

So, what do these stories teach us about the power of storytelling? They show us that storytelling is more than just a way to convey information—it's a way to connect with your audience on a deeper level, inspire action, and leave a lasting impression. By tapping into your audience's emotions, experiences, and aspirations, you can create a narrative that resonates with them and compels them to take action.

So the next time you prepare a presentation, pitch a new idea, or network at an event, don't just rely on facts and figures—tell a story. Whether it's a tale of triumph over adversity, a story of collaboration and creativity, or a narrative that touches the heart and soul, storytelling can captivate your audience and leave them wanting more. Go ahead, unleash your inner storyteller, and watch your message come to life in ways you never imagined.

Chapter 5: Skill Up Investing in Your Professional Development

The Importance of Continuous Learning and Upskilling in Today's Rapidly Evolving Job Market

Continuous learning and upskilling must be balanced in today's fast-paced and ever-evolving job market. With advancements in technology, changes in industry trends, and the rise of new skills and competencies, the work landscape constantly shifts, requiring professionals to adapt and evolve to stay relevant and competitive. Whether you're a recent graduate just starting in your career or a seasoned professional with years of experience, investing in continuous learning and upskilling is essential for staying ahead of the curve and future-proofing your career. Here's why:

Adaptability in a Rapidly Changing World: Change is the only constant in today's job market. Technologies evolve, industries transform, and job roles shift in response to emerging trends and market demands. To thrive in this dynamic environment, professionals must embrace a mindset of continuous learning and adaptation. Upskilling and staying abreast of the latest developments in your field will better equip you to navigate change, seize new opportunities, and remain agile in the face of uncertainty.

Maintaining Relevance and Competitiveness: As new technologies emerge and job roles evolve, the skills and competencies required to succeed in the workforce are constantly changing. What was considered cutting-edge just a few years ago may now be outdated. To remain relevant and competitive in your field, it's essential to continuously update and expand your skill set to align with the evolving needs of employers and the demands of the market. By investing in continuous learning and upskilling, you'll ensure that you stay ahead of the competition and position yourself as a valuable asset in the eyes of employers.

Unlocking New Opportunities for Growth: Continuous learning and upskilling help you maintain your current job and open doors to new opportunities for growth and advancement. Whether pursuing a promotion within your current organization, transitioning to a new role or industry, or launching your business venture, acquiring new skills and knowledge can broaden your horizons and expand your career prospects. By continuously investing in your professional development, you'll be better prepared to capitalize on new opportunities and advance your career.

Future-Proofing Your Career: In an era of rapid technological advancement and automation, the job market constantly evolves, and the skills in demand today may not be as relevant. By investing in continuous learning and upskilling, you'll future-proof your career and remain employable and adaptable in the face of technological disruption and industry changes. Whether learning new programming languages, acquiring digital marketing skills, or mastering data analysis techniques, staying ahead of the curve will position you for long-term success and resilience in the job market.

Personal and Professional Development: Continuous learning and upskilling benefit your career and contribute to your personal and professional development. Engaging in lifelong learning fosters intellectual curiosity, creativity, and a growth mindset, all essential for success in today's knowledge economy. By challenging yourself to acquire new skills and knowledge, you'll expand your horizons, enhance your problem-solving abilities, and become a more well-rounded and adaptable professional.

In short, the importance of continuous learning and upskilling in today's rapidly evolving job market cannot be overstated. By embracing a mindset of lifelong learning, investing in your professional development, and staying ahead of the curve, you'll position yourself for long-term success, adaptability, and resilience in the face of change. Seize every opportunity to learn, grow, and expand your skill set, and watch as your career flourishes in the dynamic and ever-evolving work landscape.

Identifying Areas for Skill Development and Finding Resources to Enhance Your Expertise
In today's competitive job market, the ability to identify areas for skill development and access resources to enhance your expertise is essential for staying relevant, advancing your career, and achieving your professional goals. Whether you're looking to strengthen your

existing skills, acquire new ones, or pivot into a different career path, countless resources are available to help you take your skills to the next level. Here's how to identify areas for skill development and find the resources you need to enhance your expertise:

Conduct a Skills Assessment: Take stock of your current skills and expertise. What are your strengths? What areas do you excel in, and where do you have room for improvement? Reflect on your experiences, colleagues' and supervisors' feedback, and any gaps you've identified in your skill set. By conducting a thorough skills assessment, you'll know where to focus your efforts and which areas to prioritize for development.

Set Clear Goals: Once you've identified areas for skill development, set clear and achievable goals for yourself. What specific skills do you want to develop or improve? What outcomes do you hope to achieve by enhancing your expertise in these areas? Whether mastering a new programming language, enhancing your communication skills, or becoming a more effective leader, setting clear goals will guide your learning journey and keep you motivated and focused.

Research Available Resources: With a clear understanding of your skill development goals, research the resources available to help you achieve them. From online courses and tutorials to books, podcasts, and workshops, countless resources are available to help you enhance your expertise in virtually any area. Look for reputable sources that align with your learning style, preferences, and budget, and be bold and explore multiple resources to find what works best for you.

Tap into Online Learning Platforms: Online learning platforms like Coursera, Udemy, LinkedIn Learning, and Skillshare offer many courses and tutorials covering various topics and skill areas. Whether you want to learn technical skills like coding and data analysis or soft skills like leadership and communication, these platforms provide convenient and accessible options for self-paced learning from industry experts and thought leaders.

Seek Out Mentorship and Coaching: Mentorship and coaching can be invaluable resources for skill development and professional growth. Contact experienced professionals in your field or within your network and inquire about mentorship opportunities or coaching services. A mentor or coach can provide guidance, feedback, and support as you work to enhance your expertise and achieve your career goals.

Network and Collaborate with Peers: Networking and collaboration with peers in your industry or field can also be valuable sources of skill development and learning. Join professional associations, attend industry events and conferences, and participate in online forums and communities to connect with like-minded professionals, share knowledge and experiences, and learn from each other's successes and challenges.

Stay Curious and Open-Minded: Stay curious and open-minded as you embark on your skill development journey. Be willing to explore new ideas, try new approaches, and step outside your comfort zone to pursue growth and learning. Embrace failure as a natural part of the learning process, and view setbacks as opportunities for growth and improvement. By approaching skill development with a mindset of curiosity and openness, you'll continuously expand your expertise and unlock new opportunities for success in your career.

By and large, identifying areas for skill development and finding resources to enhance your expertise are essential steps in advancing your career and achieving your professional goals. By conducting a skills assessment, setting clear goals, researching available resources, tapping into online learning platforms, seeking out mentorship and coaching, networking and collaborating with peers, and staying curious and open-minded, you'll be well-equipped to take your skills to the next level and thrive in today's competitive job market. Take the initiative, invest in your professional development, and watch as your expertise and opportunities for success continue to grow.

Strategies for Showcasing Your Newly Acquired Skills and Qualifications to Advance Your Career
Let's talk about how to strut your stuff and show off those newly acquired skills and qualifications like the superstar you are. In today's competitive job market, it's not enough to have the skills—you've got to know how to flaunt them in all the right ways to advance your career and stand out from the crowd. Grab your highlighter and get ready to shine bright with these hip and trendy strategies for showcasing your skills and qualifications:

Update Your Online Presence: Your online presence is your digital calling card, so make sure it's up-to-date and on point. Update your LinkedIn profile with your latest skills, certifications, and accomplishments, and make sure your resume reflects your newfound expertise. Remember to spruce up your website or portfolio to showcase your skills and projects in a visually appealing and engaging way. Remember, first impressions matter, so make sure your online presence is polished, professional, and primed to impress.

Create Compelling Content: Show off your skills and expertise by creating compelling content highlighting your knowledge and experience. Start a blog or vlog where you can share insights, tips, and tutorials related to your field. Contribute guest posts to industry publications or websites, or start a podcast where you can interview experts and share your insights. By creating valuable content that showcases your expertise, you'll position yourself as a thought leader in your field and attract attention from potential employers, clients, and collaborators.

Build a Portfolio of Projects: Put your skills into action by building a portfolio demonstrating your real-world abilities. Whether it's coding projects, design samples, marketing campaigns, or writing samples, compile a collection of your best work that showcases your skills and achievements. Remember to highlight your role in each project, the challenges you faced, and the results you achieved. A strong portfolio showcases your skills and provides tangible evidence of your abilities and accomplishments.

Network Like a Boss: Networking is critical to advancing your career and showcasing your skills to the right people. Attend industry events, conferences, and meetups to network with professionals and share your expertise. Join online communities, forums, and social media groups where you can connect with like-minded professionals and participate in discussions related to your skills and interests. Don't be afraid to put yourself out there and make meaningful connections—you never know where they might lead!

Seek Out Speaking Opportunities: Public speaking is a powerful way to showcase your expertise and build your brand. Look for opportunities to speak at conferences, workshops, webinars, or industry events where you can share your knowledge and insights with a broader audience. Prepare engaging presentations or workshops that showcase your skills and expertise, and be bold and share your personal experiences and lessons learned. Speaking engagements position you as an authority in your field and provide valuable exposure and networking opportunities.

Ask for Recommendations and Endorsements: Be bold about asking for recommendations and endorsements from colleagues, mentors, or clients who can vouch for your skills and qualifications. Contact people you've worked with and ask them to write a brief testimonial or endorse you for specific skills on LinkedIn. Positive endorsements and recommendations from others add credibility to your profile and reinforce your expertise in the eyes of potential employers or clients.

Stay Visible and Engaged: Finally, stay visible and engaged in your industry or field by staying active on social media, participating in relevant discussions and forums, and sharing interesting content related to your skills and interests. Engage with influencers, thought leaders, and industry experts, and contribute valuable insights and perspectives to the conversation. By staying visible and engaged, you'll keep your skills top of mind and position yourself as a go-to resource for all things related to your expertise.

Finally, showcasing your newly acquired skills and qualifications is essential for advancing your career and standing out in today's competitive job market. By updating your online presence, creating compelling content, building a portfolio of projects, networking like a boss, seeking out speaking opportunities, asking for recommendations and endorsements, and staying visible and engaged, you'll make sure your skills are front and center for all the right people to see. Go ahead, strut your stuff, and show the world what you're made of—you've got this!

Chapter 6: Seizing Opportunities: Saying Yes to Success

Recognizing and Capitalizing on Opportunities for Growth and Advancement

Alright, listen up, hustlers—because we're about to dive into the world of recognizing and capitalizing on opportunities for growth and advancement like the go-getters we are. In today's fast-paced and ever-evolving world, success isn't just about waiting for opportunities to come knocking—it's about spotting them from a mile away, seizing them with both hands, and riding that wave to the top. Now is a great time to grab your shades and get ready to shine because we're about to show you how it's done.

Stay Curious and Open-Minded: The first step to recognizing opportunities for growth and advancement is to stay curious and open-minded. Keep your eyes peeled for new trends, emerging technologies, and shifting market dynamics that could signal opportunities for growth in your industry or field. Be willing to step outside your comfort zone, try new things, and embrace change with open arms. Remember, fortune favors the bold, so don't fear taking risks and exploring new horizons.

Think Like an Entrepreneur: Whether you're working for a company or running your own business, thinking like an entrepreneur is crucial to spotting opportunities for growth and advancement. Look for gaps in the market, unmet needs, or untapped potential that you can leverage to create value and drive innovation. Stay nimble, agile, and ready to pivot as needed to capitalize on emerging opportunities and stay ahead of the competition.

Build Your Network: Your network is your net worth, so invest in building and nurturing relationships with people who can help you spot and capitalize on opportunities for growth and advancement. Connect with industry leaders, thought influencers, and like-minded professionals through networking events, social media, and online communities. Surround yourself with people who inspire you, challenge you, and support your goals, and don't be afraid to ask for advice, feedback, or introductions when needed.

Stay Proactive and Resourceful: Opportunities rarely fall into your lap—you've got to go out there and make them happen. Stay proactive and resourceful in seeking opportunities for growth and advancement, whether taking on new projects, pursuing additional training or certifications, or volunteering for leadership roles within your organization or community. Be proactive about seeking feedback and constructive criticism, and use it for continuous improvement and growth.

Keep Your Skills Sharp: In today's rapidly evolving job market, staying ahead of the curve requires constantly updating and expanding your skill set. Keep your skills sharp by investing in continuous learning, taking online courses, attending workshops and seminars, and seeking opportunities to gain hands-on experience in new areas. By staying at the forefront of emerging trends and technologies, you'll position yourself as a valuable asset to employers and open doors to new opportunities for advancement.

Stay Focused on Your Goals: Amid all the hustle and bustle, it's easy to lose sight of your goals and aspirations. Stay focused on your goal, and keep your eyes on the prize. Set clear, actionable goals for yourself, both short-term and long-term, and develop a roadmap for how you plan to achieve them. Break down your goals into smaller, manageable steps, and celebrate your progress. Remember, every step forward is a step closer to realizing your dreams.

Embrace Failure as a Learning Opportunity: Not every opportunity will pan out how you hoped, and that's okay. Embrace failure as a natural part of the learning process and use it as an opportunity to grow, learn, and improve. Reflect on what went wrong, extract the lessons learned, and use them to inform your future decisions and actions. Remember, it's not about how many times you fall—it's about how many times you get back up and keep pushing forward.

With this in mind, recognizing and capitalizing on opportunities for growth and advancement is essential for achieving success and reaching your full potential. By staying curious and open-minded, thinking like an entrepreneur, building your network, staying proactive and resourceful, keeping your skills sharp, staying focused on your goals, and embracing failure as a learning opportunity, you'll position yourself for success in today's competitive and ever-changing world. Seize the day and make those opportunities your own—you've got this!

Tips for Stepping Out of Your Comfort Zone, Taking Calculated Risks, and Embracing New Challenges
Alright, listen up, hustlers, because we're about to dive into the world of stepping out of your comfort zone, taking calculated risks, and embracing new challenges like the fearless pioneers we are. In today's fast-paced and ever-evolving world, success isn't just about playing it safe—it's about pushing the boundaries, taking chances, and daring to be bold. Grab your favorite sneakers and get ready to enter the unknown because I'll show you how to break free from the status quo and unleash your full potential.

Embrace the Uncomfortable: Let's face it—growth doesn't happen in the comfort zone. It's time to embrace the uncomfortable, lean into the unknown, and get comfortable with being uncomfortable. Whether speaking up in a meeting, volunteering for a challenging project, or pursuing a new career path, don't let fear hold you back from taking risks and seizing new opportunities. Remember, the magic happens outside your comfort zone, so embrace the discomfort and watch as your confidence and capabilities soar to new heights.

Start Small and Build Momentum: Stepping out of your comfort zone doesn't have to mean jumping headfirst into the deep end. Start small and build momentum by taking incremental steps outside your comfort zone. It could be trying a new hobby, experimenting with a different communication style, or introducing yourself to someone new at a networking event. Whatever it is, start with small, manageable challenges and gradually work your way up to bigger ones. Each small victory will give you the confidence and courage to tackle even more significant challenges.

Flip the Script on Fear: Fear is a natural response to the unknown but doesn't have to hold you back. Instead of letting fear control you, flip the script and use it as fuel for growth and transformation. Embrace fear as a sign that you're on the right track—pushing yourself beyond your limits and daring to be great. Channel that fear into action, and let it propel you forward rather than hold you back. Remember, fear is just a feeling—what you do in the face of fear genuinely matters.

Visualize Success: Visualization is a powerful tool for overcoming fear and building confidence. Take a moment to visualize yourself succeeding in the face of new challenges. Picture yourself confidently tackling obstacles, overcoming setbacks, and quickly achieving your goals. Visualize the positive outcomes and rewards that await you on the other side of fear. By visualizing success, you'll rewire your brain to focus on the possibilities rather than the limitations and empower yourself to take bold action to pursue your dreams.

Seek Support and Accountability: You don't have to go it alone—seek support and accountability from friends, family, or colleagues who can cheer you on and hold you accountable as you step out of your comfort zone. Share your goals and challenges with trusted allies who can offer encouragement, advice, and support. Whether it's joining a mastermind group, enlisting the help of a mentor, or partnering with a buddy to tackle challenges, having a support system can make all the difference in helping you stay motivated and on track.

Learn from Failure and Adapt: Stepping out of your comfort zone inevitably comes with its fair share of failures and setbacks, and that's okay. Instead of letting failure discourage you, use it as a learning opportunity to grow and adapt. Reflect on what went wrong, extract the lessons learned, and apply them to your next attempt. Remember, failure is not the end—it's just a detour on the road to success. Keep pushing, learning, and growing, and do not let setbacks derail your journey to greatness.

Celebrate Your Victories: Remember to celebrate your victories, no matter how small. Every step outside your comfort zone is a win worth celebrating, so take the time to acknowledge and appreciate your progress. Whether treating yourself to a special reward, sharing your achievements with loved ones, or simply patting yourself on the back, celebrate your courage and resilience in stepping outside your comfort zone. Celebrating your victories will reinforce positive behaviors and build momentum for future success.

The bottom line is stepping out of your comfort zone, taking calculated risks, and embracing new challenges, essential for personal and professional growth. By embracing the uncomfortable, starting small and building momentum, flipping the script on fear, visualizing success, seeking support and accountability, learning from failure and adapting, and celebrating your victories, you'll unleash your full potential and achieve greatness beyond your wildest dreams. Go ahead, take that leap of faith, and watch as the world opens up to you in ways you never imagined. You've got this!

Strategies for Advocating for Yourself and Negotiating Promotions, Raises, and Career Advancement Opportunities
If you haven't strapped in already, now is a good time to do so because we're about to dive into the world of advocating for yourself and negotiating like a boss to secure the promotions, raises, and career advancement opportunities you deserve. In today's fast-paced and ever-evolving workplace, it's not just about working hard—it's about knowing your worth, speaking up for yourself, and negotiating with confidence and swagger. Grab your favorite power suit and get ready to channel your inner negotiator because I'm about to lay down some strategies for making moves and taking your career to the next level.

Know Your Worth: The first step to advocating for yourself and negotiating like a pro is knowing your worth. Take the time to research industry standards, market trends, and salary benchmarks for your role and level of experience. Know what you bring to the table—your skills, accomplishments, and unique value proposition—and be prepared to articulate them confidently and convincingly. Remember, you're not just asking for what you want—you're advocating for your worth.

Be Confident and Assertive. Confidence is crucial in advocating for yourself and negotiating with employers. Walk into that negotiation room (or virtual meeting) with your head held high, your shoulders back, and your confidence radiating from every pore. Speak assertively and confidently, and don't be afraid to assert your value and express your needs and expectations. Confidence is contagious; others will, too, when you believe in yourself.

Prepare, Prepare, Prepare: The key to successful negotiation is preparation. Take the time to prepare your talking points, gather evidence to support your case, and anticipate potential objections or pushback. Practice your pitch until it rolls off your tongue effortlessly, and be ready to respond to any curve balls that come your way. The more prepared you are, the more confident and in control you'll feel during the negotiation process.

Lead with Value: When advocating for yourself, focus on your value and how it benefits the organization. Highlight your accomplishments, contributions, and impact on the company's bottom line, and make a compelling case for why you deserve that promotion, raise, or career advancement opportunity. Show them the money—literally—and clarify that investing in you is a wise business decision that will pay dividends in the long run.

Be Flexible and Creative: Negotiation involves finding common ground and reaching a mutually beneficial agreement. Be willing to be flexible and creative in your negotiations and explore alternative options or compromises that meet your and the company's needs. It could be negotiating for additional benefits or perks, like flexible hours, remote work opportunities, or professional development opportunities. Or it's negotiating for a phased approach to your promotion or raise, with clear milestones and targets to measure your progress. Whatever it is, be open to exploring creative solutions that satisfy both parties and move the conversation forward.

Stay Calm and Collected: Negotiation can be nerve-wracking, but it's essential to stay calm, relaxed, and collected under pressure. Keep your emotions in check, and resist the urge to react impulsively or defensively to pushback or counteroffers. Stay focused on your objectives, and approach the negotiation with a clear head and a positive attitude. Remember, negotiation is a game of strategy and persuasion; staying calm and collected will give you the upper hand in the negotiation room.

Follow-Up and Follow-Through: Follow up on any agreements or commitments once the negotiation ends. Send a thank-you note to express your appreciation for the opportunity to discuss your career advancement and confirm any next steps or action items agreed upon during the negotiation. Stay proactive in following up on your progress and holding yourself and others accountable for delivering on their promises. Demonstrating your professionalism and commitment to your goals will leave a lasting impression and set you up for continued success in your career.

Advocating for yourself and negotiating promotions, raises, and career advancement opportunities are essential for taking control of your career and achieving your professional goals. By knowing your worth, being confident and assertive, preparing thoroughly, leading with value, being flexible and creative, staying calm and collected, following up and following through, you'll position yourself for success and ensure you're compensated and recognized for your hard work and contributions. Go ahead, make it do what it do, and negotiate like your boss—you've got this!

Chapter 7: Hustle with Purpose: Finding Meaning in Your Career Journey

Aligning Your Career Goals with Your Values and Passions to Create a Fulfilling Professional Life

Let's talk about creating a career that's not just about punching the clock but about living your best life and making moves that align with your values and passions. In today's fast-paced and ever-evolving world, it's not enough to just chase the paycheck—you've got to chase your dreams, follow your passions, and build a career that lights you up from the inside out. It's time to grab your favorite latte and get ready to vibe with these tips for aligning your career goals with your values and passions to create a fulfilling professional life.

Get Clear on Your Values: The first step to creating a fulfilling career is getting clear on your values—who you are, what you stand for, and what matters most to you. Take some time to reflect on what truly drives and motivates you personally and professionally. Is it creativity, innovation, social impact, work-life balance, or something else? Once you've identified your core values, use them as a guiding light to inform your career decisions and align your goals with what truly matters to you.

Follow Your Passions: Life's too short to spend it doing work that doesn't light you up and set your soul on fire. Identify your passions—those that energize, inspire, and make you come alive—and find ways to incorporate them into your career. Whether pursuing a career in a field you're passionate about, starting your own business based on your interests, or finding ways to bring your passions into your current role, make sure your career reflects who you are and what you love.

Set Meaningful Goals: Once you've identified your values and passions, set meaningful goals that align with them. What do you want to achieve in your career? What impact do you want to make? Set specific, measurable, achievable, relevant, and time-bound (SMART) goals that reflect your values and passions and inspire you to take action. Whether landing your dream job, starting your own business, or making a difference in your community, ensure your goals align with what truly matters to you.

Seek Out Purposeful Work: Purpose is the secret sauce that turns a job into a calling—a paycheck into a passion. Seek out work that aligns with your values and allows you to make a meaningful impact on the world around you. Look for companies, organizations, or roles that share your values and offer opportunities for growth, fulfillment, and purposeful work. Whether working for a mission-driven organization, volunteering for a cause you're passionate about, or starting your social enterprise, find ways to infuse purpose into your career and make a positive difference in the world.

Stay Authentic and True to Yourself: In a constantly changing and evolving world, it's easy to get caught up in chasing external validation and approval. But true fulfillment comes from staying authentic and genuine to yourself—embracing who you are, what you believe in, and what makes you unique. Don't be afraid to march to the beat of your drum, follow your intuition, and chart your course, even if it means going against the grain or taking the road less traveled. Your authenticity is your greatest asset, so embrace it wholeheartedly and let it shine through in everything you do.

Find Balance and Harmony: Creating a fulfilling career isn't just about achieving professional success—it's about finding balance and harmony in all areas of your life. Prioritize self-care, work-life balance, and personal well-being, and make sure your career goals are in harmony with your overall lifestyle and priorities. Whether spending time with loved ones, pursuing hobbies and interests outside of work, or taking time for self-reflection and personal growth, ensure your career supports and enhances your overall well-being and happiness.

Stay Open to Opportunities: Finally, stay open to opportunities and embrace the unexpected twists and turns that come your way. Life is full of surprises, and you must always determine where the next opportunity might lead. Stay curious, adventurous, and open-minded, and be willing to explore new possibilities and take calculated risks to pursue your goals and passions. Keep an open heart and mind, and trust that the universe has your back as you navigate your career journey.

In conclusion, aligning your career goals with your values and passions is essential for creating a fulfilling professional life that lights you up and brings you joy. By getting clear on your values, following your passions, setting meaningful goals, seeking out purposeful work, staying authentic and genuine to yourself, finding balance and harmony, and staying open to opportunities, you'll create a career that's not just a job, but a calling—a journey of self-discovery, growth, and fulfillment. Go ahead, dream big, follow your heart, and create the career of your dreams—you've got this!

Tips for Maintaining Work-Life Balance and Avoiding Burnout While Hustling Toward Your Goals

Alright, listen up, hustlers, because I'm about to drop some profound knowledge on how to maintain that work-life balance and avoid burning out while you're out there hustling toward your goals like the rockstar you are. In today's fast-paced and hyper-connected world, it's easy to get caught up in the hustle and grind, but it's essential to remember that balance is critical to long-term success and happiness. Grab your favorite smoothie and get ready to vibe with these tips for keeping cool and staying sane while you hustle toward your goals.

Set Boundaries: The first rule of maintaining work-life balance is setting boundaries—knowing when to say "yes" and "no" to work and personal commitments. Establish clear boundaries around your work hours, downtime, and personal time, and stick to them like your favorite playlist. Learn to prioritize your time and energy on the things that matter most to you, and don't be afraid to say no to things that don't align with your goals or values. Remember, boundaries are your best friend when maintaining balance in your life.

Schedule Self-Care: Self-care isn't just a buzzword—it's non-negotiable for maintaining your sanity and well-being in the hustle and bustle of everyday life. Make self-care a priority by scheduling regular time for activities that nourish your mind, body, and soul. Whether hitting the gym, practicing mindfulness and meditation, indulging in a spa day, or simply walking in nature, make time for activities that recharge your batteries and rejuvenate your spirit. Remember, you can't pour from an empty cup, so prioritize self-care like your life depends on it—because it does.

Work Smarter, Not Harder: In the age of hustle culture, it's easy to fall into the trap of working harder, not more intelligent—but that's a recipe for burnout, not success. Instead of burning the midnight oil and grinding yourself into the ground, focus on working smarter, not harder. Prioritize your tasks based on their importance and urgency, delegate or outsource tasks when possible, and use tools and technology to streamline your workflow and increase efficiency.

Remember, it's not about how many hours you put in—it's about what you accomplish with your time.

Disconnect and Unplug: In today's hyper-connected world, it's easy to feel like you have to be available 24/7—but that's a one-way ticket to burn-out-ville. Make a conscious effort to disconnect and unplug from work when you're off the clock. Set boundaries around your screen time, turn off notifications, and resist the urge to check your email or social media during downtime. Give yourself permission to truly disconnect and be present at the moment, whether you're spending time with loved ones, pursuing hobbies, or simply enjoying some much-needed R&R. Remember, life is happening in the here and now—don't miss out on it because you're glued to your screen.

Delegate and Outsource: You don't have to do it all yourself—learn to delegate and outsource tasks to free up your time and energy for the things that matter most to you. Whether hiring a virtual assistant to handle administrative tasks, outsourcing household chores, or enlisting the help of friends and family, don't be afraid to ask for help when needed. Remember, you're not superhuman, and it's okay to lean on others for support and assistance when you're feeling overwhelmed. Delegate like a boss and watch your stress levels plummet as you reclaim your time and sanity.

Practice Mindfulness and Gratitude: Amid the hustle and grind, it's easy to lose sight of the present moment and get caught up in worries about the future or regrets about the past. Mindfulness and gratitude can help you stay grounded, centered, and present in the here and now. Take time daily to practice mindfulness meditation, deep breathing, or other relaxation techniques to quiet your mind and reduce stress. Cultivate an attitude of gratitude by focusing on what you're thankful for in your life, whether it's your health, your relationships, or the simple pleasures of everyday life. Remember, happiness is found in the present moment—so don't let it slip away while you're busy chasing your dreams.

Make Time for Fun and Play: Last but not least, remember to make time for fun and play in your life. Remember what it's like to be a kid again—uninhibited, carefree, and joyful. Whether playing sports, dancing like nobody's watching, or indulging in your favorite hobbies and interests, make time for activities that bring you joy and make your heart sing. Remember, life's too short to take too seriously—so laugh often, play hard, and don't forget to have fun along the way.

To put it bluntly, maintaining work-life balance and avoiding burnout while hustling toward your goals is essential for long-term success and happiness. By setting boundaries, scheduling self-care, working smarter, not harder, disconnecting and unplugging, delegating and outsourcing, practicing mindfulness and gratitude, and making time for fun and play, you'll keep your cool and stay sane in the hustle and bustle of everyday life. Go ahead, hustle hard, but don't forget to care for yourself along the way—you've got this!

Strategies for Giving Back and Using Your Skills and Influence to Make a Positive Impact On Your Community and Beyond

Listen up, changemakers, because we're about to dive into the world of giving back and using your skills and influence to positively impact your community and beyond like the superhero you are. In today's fast-paced and ever-evolving world, it's not just about chasing success—it's about using your power and influence for good, making a difference in the lives of others, and leaving a positive legacy that extends far beyond your achievements. Grab your cape and get ready to save the day because I'm about to lay down some trendy strategies for improving the world, one act of kindness at a time.

Volunteer Your Time and Talent: The first step to giving back is to roll up your sleeves and get involved in your community. Find a cause or organization near and dear to your heart, whether supporting underserved communities, protecting the environment, or promoting education and literacy, and volunteer your time and talent to make a difference. Use your skills, expertise, and influence to lend a helping hand, whether mentoring at-risk youth, organizing fundraising events, or using your platform to raise awareness for critical issues. Remember, giving back isn't just about writing a check—it's about rolling up your sleeves and getting your hands dirty to create meaningful change in the world.

Pay It Forward: One of the simplest and most powerful ways to make a positive impact is to pay it forward—performing acts of kindness and generosity without expecting anything in return. Whether buying a stranger's coffee, leaving a generous tip for your server, or helping a neighbor in need, look for opportunities to spread kindness and positivity wherever you go. Remember, small acts of kindness can ripple out and create a wave of goodness that touches countless lives. Be the change you wish to see in the world, and watch as your kindness comes back to you tenfold.

Use Your Influence for Good: As someone with skills and influence, you can amplify your impact and drive positive change on a larger scale. Use your platform, whether social media, professional network, or community connections, to raise awareness for important causes and advocate for meaningful change. Share your knowledge, expertise, and passion with others, and use your voice to speak up for those who may not have a voice. Remember, with great power comes great responsibility, so use your influence wisely and make a positive impact wherever you go.

Support Causes You Believe In: Another powerful way to give back is to support causes and organizations that align with your values and passions. Whether donating to a nonprofit organization, sponsoring a fundraising event, or participating in a charity run or walk, find ways to support causes near and dear to your heart. Look for opportunities to make a meaningful impact, whether it's through financial contributions, volunteer work, or advocacy efforts. Remember, every dollar you donate, every hour you volunteer, and every voice you raise makes a difference in the lives of others.

Lead by Example: Finally, lead by example and inspire others to join you to make a positive impact. Be a role model for kindness, compassion, and generosity, and show others what it means to be a changemaker. Share your experiences, successes, and challenges with others, and encourage them to join you in your efforts to give back and make a difference. Remember, the power of one person to create change is immense—but the power of many working together is unstoppable. Lead by example, and watch as your actions inspire others to follow suit and join you in your mission to improve the world.

The bottom line is that giving back and using your skills and influence to impact your community positively and beyond is essential for creating a better world for future generations. By volunteering your time and talent, paying it forward, using your influence for good, supporting causes you believe in, and leading by example, you'll leave a lasting legacy far beyond your lifetime. Go ahead, be the change you wish to see in the world and watch your acts of kindness and generosity ripple out and create a wave of goodness that touches countless lives. You've got the power to change the world—so what are you waiting for? Let's make a difference!

Conclusion:

Recap of Key Takeaways and Actionable Steps For Scaling Your Career Growth Through Strategic Promotion Strategies

It's time to wrap things up and leave you with some significant keys for scaling your career growth through strategic promotion strategies like the boss you are. We've covered a lot of ground, from hustling like a pro to advocating for yourself, building your brand, and giving back to your community. Now it's time to distill all that wisdom into some actionable steps that you can take to level up your career and achieve the success you deserve. Grab your notebook and pen because I will drop some serious knowledge bombs.

Know Your Worth and Own It: The first step to scaling your career growth is knowing your worth and owning it like a boss. Take the time to identify your skills, accomplishments, and unique value proposition, and don't be afraid to shout it from the rooftops. Remember, no one else will if you don't believe in yourself. Embrace your strengths, own your achievements, and show the world what you're made of.

Set Ambitious Yet Achievable Goals: Next up, set ambitious yet achievable goals that align with your values, passions, and aspirations. Whether landing that dream job, earning that promotion, or starting your own business, set clear, actionable goals that inspire you to take action and push yourself to new heights. Break down your goals into smaller, manageable steps, and create a roadmap for how to achieve them. Remember, every journey starts with a single step—so take that first step and keep hustling until you reach your destination.

Build Your Brand: Your brand is your secret weapon for standing out in a crowded marketplace and attracting opportunities like a magnet. Take the time to define your brand—who you are, what you stand for, and what makes you unique—and showcase it proudly to the world. Whether through your resume, LinkedIn profile, or online portfolio, ensure your brand shines through in everything you do. Remember, your brand is your calling card, so make it count.

Network Like a Boss: They say your network is your net worth, and they couldn't be more suitable. Building and nurturing genuine relationships with industry peers, mentors, and potential collaborators is essential for scaling your career growth and unlocking new opportunities. Get out there and network like a boss—attend networking events, join professional organizations, and leverage social media to connect with like-minded professionals in your field. Remember, relationships are the currency of success, so invest in them wisely.

Advocate for Yourself: Don't wait for opportunities to come knocking—go out there and create them yourself. Advocate for yourself, speak up for what you want, and don't be afraid to negotiate for promotions, raises, and career advancement opportunities. Remember, if you don't ask, you don't get it. So, channel your inner negotiator, know your worth, and don't settle for anything less than you deserve.

Stay Resilient and Keep Hustling: Last but not least, stay resilient and keep hustling, even when the going gets tough. Remember, success is not a straight line—it's a journey full of ups and downs, twists and turns. So, stay resilient in the face of obstacles, learn from failure, and keep pushing forward no matter what. Remember, the road to success is paved with hard work, determination, and a lot of hustle—so keep hustling until you reach the top.

In short, scaling your career growth through strategic promotion strategies is about knowing your worth, setting ambitious goals, building your brand, networking like a boss, advocating for yourself, and staying resilient in the face of adversity. These key takeaways and actionable steps will position you for success and advance your career. Go ahead, seize the day, and make those promotion dreams a reality—you've got this!

A Final Pep Talk to Keep the Hustle Alive, Stay Inspired, and Continue Pursuing Your Dreams with Passion and Determination

Alright, hustlers, gather around because it's time for one final pep talk to keep that hustle alive and inspire you to continue pursuing your dreams with passion, purpose, and relentless determination. We've covered a lot of ground on this journey—from setting goals to building your brand, networking like a pro, and advocating for yourself like a boss. But now it's time to dig deep, find that inner fire, and keep pushing forward, no matter what obstacles come your way.

Listen up because here's the truth: the road to success is not for the faint of heart. It's a journey full of twists and turns, ups and downs, highs and lows. But here's the thing: every setback is just a setup for a comeback. Every failure is just a stepping stone on the path to greatness. Don't let fear hold you back, don't let doubt dim your shine, or let anyone tell you that you can't achieve your dreams.

You've got the skills, the passion, and the drive to make it happen. You've worked, honed your craft, and hustled harder than anyone else in the game. Don't stop now. Keep grinding, hustling, and pushing yourself to new heights of greatness.

Remember, success is not a destination—it's a journey. It's not about reaching some arbitrary finish line—it's about embracing the process, enjoying the ride, and becoming the best version of yourself. Don't get discouraged by the setbacks, the rejections, or the naysayers. Use them as fuel to propel you forward, push you harder, and inspire you to reach for the stars.

And when you feel like giving up—when the hustle feels too hard, the road too long, and the dream too far away—remember why you started. Remember the passion that burns inside you, the purpose that drives you, and the vision that fuels your ambition. Hold onto that fire, that spark, that inner light, and let it guide you through the darkness.

Because here's the thing: you can achieve anything you want. You have the power to change your life, to make a difference in the world, and to leave a legacy that will inspire others for generations to come. Don't let anyone dim your shine, don't let anyone hold you back, and don't let anyone tell you that you can't do it.

You've got this. You've always had it. Seize the day, and realize your dreams. The world is yours for the taking. Keep hustling, grinding, and shining bright like the supernova you are. The world is waiting for you to make your mark—so go out there and leave a legacy that will last a lifetime. You've got this: peace out, hustlers.

Encouragement to Stay Connected and Share Their Success Stories with The Hustle Community

Hey there, hustlers! It's time to keep the vibe alive and stay connected with your fellow movers and shakers in the hustle community. We've all been on this journey together—grinding, hustling, and chasing our dreams with passion and determination. But here's the thing: we're stronger together. Let's keep that connection alive and inspire each other to greatness.

Listen up because here's the deal: success is not a solo sport—it's a team effort. We rise by lifting others, sharing our stories, and celebrating each other's wins. Let's stay connected and keep that hustle community vibe strong.

Here's the truth: your success story is not just about you—it's about inspiring others to believe in themselves, to chase their dreams, and never to give up. Don't be shy—share your wins, victories, and triumphs with the hustle community. Whether it's landing that dream job, launching that passion project, or hitting that major milestone, let us celebrate with you and cheer you every step of the way.

And remember, it's not just about the big wins—it's about the small victories too. Whether overcoming a setback, learning a new skill, or stepping out of your comfort zone, every step forward is worth celebrating. Let's keep that positive energy flowing and inspire each other to greatness.

Let's keep that hustle community vibe alive and inspire others to greatness. Whether through social media, networking events, or good old-fashioned face-to-face conversations, let's stay connected and share our stories with the world.

And remember, the hustle community is not just about celebrating success—it's about supporting each other through the tough times, too. Let's be there for each other, lend a helping hand when needed, and lift each other when the going gets tough.

Lastly, we're stronger together. The world is waiting for us to make our mark. Let's go out there and show it what we're made of. Peace out, hustlers!

Appendix

Additional Resources:

LinkedIn Learning: Access thousands of courses taught by industry experts on topics ranging from leadership and communication to technical skills and personal development.

Coursera: Explore courses and specializations from top universities and companies worldwide, covering everything from business and technology to data science and healthcare.

Udemy: Discover affordable courses on various topics, including career development, entrepreneurship, marketing, and more.

Skillshare: Join a creative community of learners and explore classes on design, photography, writing, and other creative skills to enhance your career.

TED Talks: Watch inspiring talks by thought leaders and innovators on topics related to career growth, personal development, leadership, and more.

Podcasts: Listen to podcasts hosted by industry experts and successful entrepreneurs for insights, advice, and inspiration on navigating your career journey.

Recommended Reading:

Atomic Habits by James Clear: This practical guide to personal development will help you build better habits, make meaningful changes, and achieve your goals.

Grit: The Power of Passion and Perseverance by Angela Duckworth: Discover the importance of grit—passion, and perseverance—for achieving long-term success in your career and life.

The 7 Habits of Highly Effective People by Stephen R. Covey: Explore timeless principles for personal and professional effectiveness that will empower you to take control of your life and achieve your goals.

Lean In: Women, Work, and the Will to Lead by Sheryl Sandberg: Gain insights and practical advice for women navigating workplace challenges and leaning into their ambitions.

Start with Why: How Great Leaders Inspire Everyone to Take Action by Simon Sinek: Learn how to articulate your purpose and inspire others to follow you by understanding the importance of starting with why.

Crucial Conversations: Tools for Talking When Stakes Are High by Kerry Patterson, Joseph Grenny, Ron McMillan, and Al Switzler: Master the art of having difficult conversations and communicating effectively in personal and professional settings.

Tools for Career Growth:

Asana: Stay organized and manage your tasks, projects, and goals with this powerful project management tool.

Trello: Visualize your workflow, collaborate with team members, and stay on top of your projects with this flexible project management tool.

Evernote: This versatile note-taking app lets you capture ideas, take notes, and stay organized across all your devices.

Google Workspace: Collaborate with colleagues, store files securely, and communicate effectively with Gmail, Google Drive, Google Docs, and other productivity tools.

Slack: Stay connected with your team, collaborate in real-time, and streamline communication with this popular messaging app for businesses.

Canva: This easy-to-use design tool creates professional-looking graphics, presentations, and marketing materials.

These resources, recommended reading, and tools are here to support you on your career growth journey. Whether you're looking to develop new skills, gain inspiration, or streamline your workflow, these resources have covered you. Go ahead, dive in, and take your career to new heights!

Inspirational Quotes:

"The only way to do great work is to love what you do." - **Steve Jobs.**

"Success is not final, failure is not fatal: It is the courage to continue that count." - **Winston Churchill.**

"The only limit to our realization of tomorrow will be our doubts of today." - **Franklin D. Roosevelt.**

"The future belongs to those who believe in the beauty of their dreams." - **Eleanor Roosevelt.**

"The only person you are destined to become is the person you decide to be." - **Ralph Waldo Emerson.**

"Don't watch the clock; do what it does. Keep going." - **Sam Levenson.**

Success Stories:

Sara Blakely - Founder of Spanx: Sara Blakely started Spanx with just $5,000 and a bold idea to revolutionize women's undergarments. Today, Spanx is a billion-dollar company, and Sara is one of the most successful female entrepreneurs in the world.

Elon Musk, CEO of SpaceX and Tesla, is known for his ambitious goals and relentless determination to change the world. From building electric cars to colonizing Mars, Musk has proven that anything is possible with vision, perseverance, and hustle.

Oprah Winfrey - Media Mogul and Philanthropist: From humble beginnings, Oprah Winfrey rose to become one of the world's most influential and successful women. Through her talk show, media empire, and philanthropic efforts, Oprah has inspired millions to live their best lives and make a difference in the world.

Jeff Bezos - Founder of Amazon: Jeff Bezos started Amazon as an online bookstore in his garage. Today, Amazon is the largest online retailer in the world, and Bezos is one of the wealthiest people on the planet. His story is a testament to the power of innovation, persistence, and a willingness to take risks.

J.K. Rowling - Author of the Harry Potter series: J.K. Rowling went from being a struggling single mother living on welfare to one of the best-selling authors of all time. Her Harry Potter series has sold over 500 million copies worldwide and inspired a generation of readers to believe in the magic of storytelling.

Dwayne "The Rock" Johnson - Actor and Entrepreneur: Dwayne Johnson went from being a professional wrestler to one of the highest-paid actors in Hollywood. His journey is a testament to the power of hard work, perseverance, and never giving up on your dreams.

These inspirational quotes and success stories remind you that anything is possible with vision, determination, and hustle. So keep pushing forward, chasing your dreams, and never stop believing in yourself. The world is waiting for you to make your mark, so go out there and show it what you're made of!

The Author:

Hello there! I'm Patrick Hart

From humble beginnings to boardroom triumphs, Patrick embodies the essence of resilience and determination. As a U.S. Veteran, I learned the value of discipline, leadership, and tenacity. These qualities have been the backbone of my journey, guiding me from a childhood defined by poverty to a life of professional success and financial stability.

With a Master's Degree in Management in hand, I embarked on a career that saw me rise through the healthcare industry ranks. My tenure as a Healthcare Executive was marked by strategic vision and transformative leadership. I was privileged to be part of a dynamic leadership team that steered a pioneering Healthcare Technology Company to unprecedented heights. Our efforts culminated in the sale of the company for a record-breaking sum, a testament to our innovative approach and relentless pursuit of excellence.

But my story isn't just about financial success—it's about breaking barriers and setting new standards. Growing up, the odds were stacked against me. Yet, I carved out a path to prosperity through grit, education, and an unwavering belief in the power of change. My experiences in the military and the corporate world have imbued me with a unique perspective on what it takes to succeed in any arena.

Today, I am passionate about sharing my journey and the lessons learned along the way. Whether through speaking engagements, mentorship, or this book, my goal is to inspire others to defy their circumstances and achieve their dreams. My story is a testament to the idea that anything is possible with vision, hard work, and the right opportunities.